GARY JONES

Tallinn

First edition

This book was professionally typeset on Reedsy.
Find out more at reedsy.com

Contents

Introduction

You may have already visited or still planning to visit popular European cities like London, Paris, or Rome. But, you must not miss your chance to visit Tallinn.

Lonely Planet named Tallinn as the Best Value Destination of 2018. It is also a UNESCO World Heritage Site. It is an Estonian city where you will find amazing historical sites and modern establishments.

Tallinn has a lot to offer especially for tourists who want an experience like no other. Estonians welcome guests with their rich culture through various events, foods, and activities.

It is also a very accessible city. It would only take a few hours to reach Tallinn from most European cities. You can easily go around the city on foot, by bike, or by their reliable transport systems.

If you are planning on visiting Tallinn, it is important that you are equipped with enough knowledge of the city to make the most out of your trip.

In this guide, you will learn about the most popular activities and destinations in Tallinn. There are lists of the best restaurants, affordable hotels, museums, nightclubs, and more. You will also find an itinerary for a 3-day visit in Tallinn, important tips, and detailed information on how to get around the city.

So before packing those bags, take time to read through this travel guide on how you can maximize your 3-day stay in Tallinn and learn about what you can expect from this wonderful Estonian city.

1

Tallinn's Brief History and Background

The Early History

Evidence of human settlement in Tallinn was found in the region of Iru which dated in the 9th-10th century AD. Though, many thought that human existence in Tallinn started about 5,000 years ago.

On Toompea Hill, the first fortress was built and was used until the 11th century AD. It was once conquered by the King of Denmark Valdemar II's crusaders and by the Brothers of the Sword.

The Danish ruled over Tallinn from 1219 to 1346. Since the start of their rule, Tallinn was known as Reval and the city's history has been more documented. The German Teutonic Knights bought Tallinn from the Danish in 1346.

There is a legend that the Danish Flag or the Danneborg fell into Tallinn's King's Garden in 1219 which was adopted as the Flag of Denmark. If the legend was true, it would be the World's Oldest Used Flag. Tallinn also used the Danneborg as one of its coat of arms.

The 14th to 16th Centuries

The majority of Tallinn's town center was constructed between the14th and 16th centuries.

During this time, Tallinn played an important role as a trading capital. In 1561, Tallinn was governed by the Swedish until the Great Northern War where the Russians took over in 1710.

World Wars 1 and 2

Russia ruled over Estonia during World War 1 until the 1917 Russian Revolution. Estonia grabbed this chance to proclaim its independence on February 24, 1918. The "Tartu Peace Treaty" was created after two years of an independence war with Russia. The treaty was Russia's formal acknowledgment of Estonia's independence.

When World War 2 started, Tallinn was once again occupied by Russia. But, Germany invaded the city in August 1941. Estonia became the Nazis' base for many extermination camps where an estimated 10,000 Jews from Estonia and neighboring countries were killed.

The Germans left Estonia in 1944 and once again, the Soviets ruled over the country where they remained for many years.

The Independence of Estonia

The country was renamed from "The Estonian Soviet Socialist Republic" to "The Republic of Estonia" in May 1990. The Soviet Union recognized Estonia's independence on September 6, 1991. This was also when Tallinn became the capital of the country.

Since their independence, Estonia became one of the most successful countries in the European Union in terms of economic status.

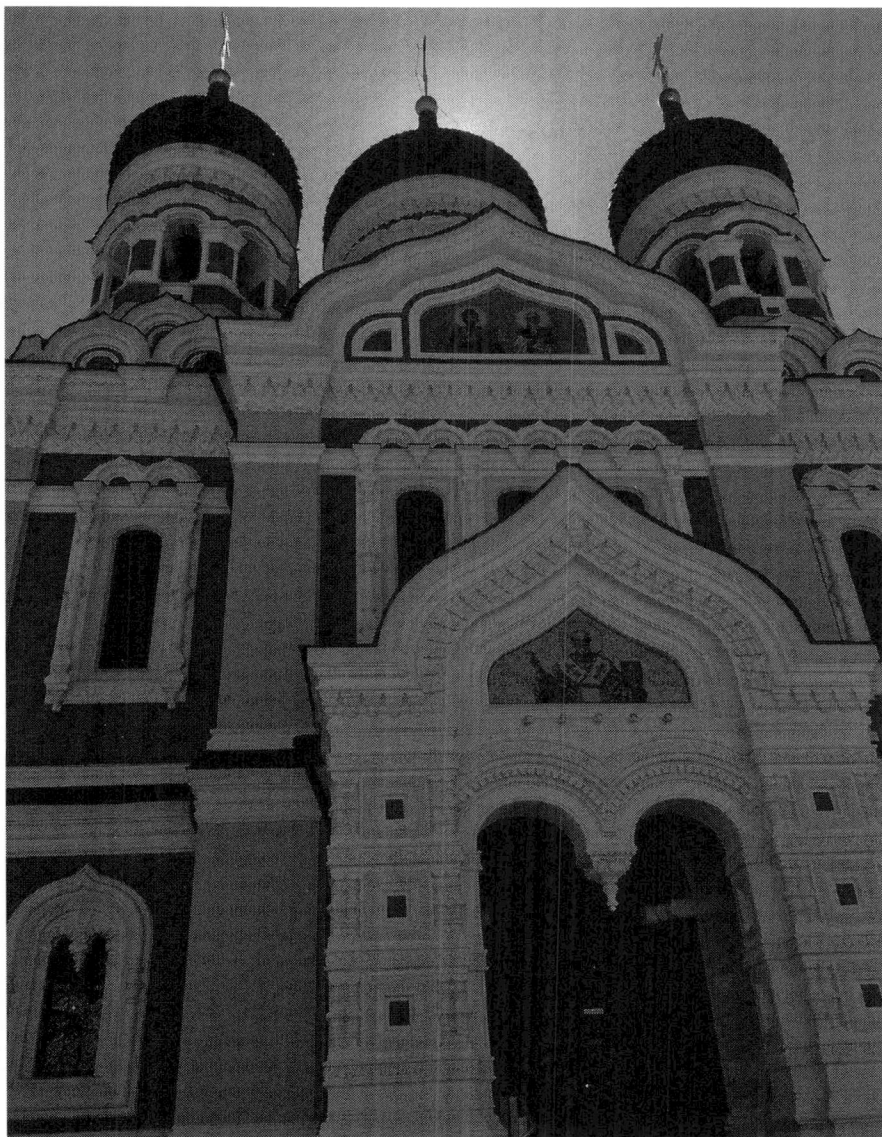

2

The Best Time to Visit Tallinn

The best time to visit Tallinn would depend on the activities you would like to do and the kind of weather you are used to.

If you are traveling on a budget, you may want to avoid going to Tallinn on June, April, and September. These are the busiest months for tourism in the city. Expect hotels and flight prices to be much more expensive during these months.

The month with the least tourist visits is February. But, you may not enjoy the weather during this month if you are not used to extremely cold winters.

Tallinn Weather by Season

Winter (December-February)

Travelers who are used to warm weather would not enjoy winter in Tallinn. Temperature during this season can go as low as 37.4°F to 26.2°F and it may rain or snow 4-10 times a month. Because of this, many tourists avoid Tallinn during winter.

But, you can still enjoy different fun activities in Tallinn during winter like skiing, ice skating, and ice fishing.

Spring (March-May)

Temperature during spring ranges from 67.1°F and 35.2°F. It may rain for 4-5 days a month. This season is the 2nd busiest time for tourism in Tallinn due to the great weather for various activities.

This is the best season for touring around the city and enjoying the great outdoors.

Summer (June-August)

Summer is the busiest time for Tallinn tourism because of the cool and comfortable weather. Temperatures may range from 48.2°F to 71.6°F with moderate precipitation. Accommodation and other tourism services usually cost more during this season.

During summer, expect famous tourist spots to be busy and hotels to be fully-booked. It is advisable that you book your hotel earlier if you are visiting Tallinn in summer.

Autumn (June-August)

You will find delight in the cool weather during autumn in Tallinn because of the wind and humidity. Temperature ranges from 65.1°F and 36.9°F. It may rain or snow 7-9 days a month which make this season slow on tourism. Accommodation and tourism services may cost lower during these months.

Still, there are many enjoyable activities you can do in Tallinn during autumn.

3

Tallinn Transportation

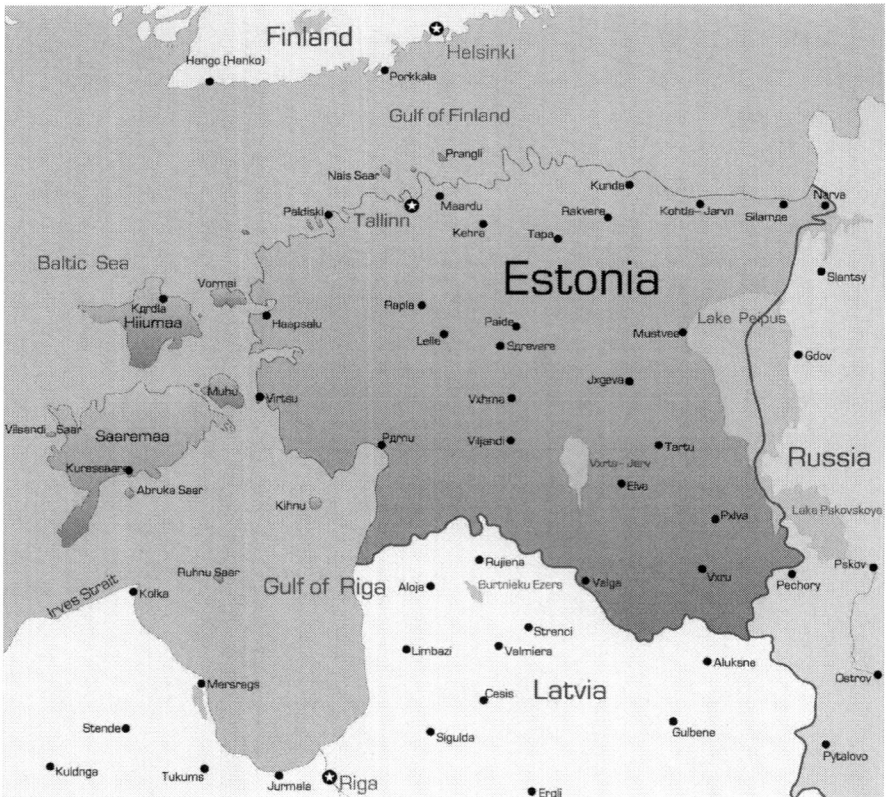

Getting to Tallinn

If you are flying into Tallinn, you will land on Tallinn Airport (Lennart Meri Tallinn Airport). It is only 2 miles away from Raekoja Plats (Town Hall Square). From the airport, you can take a tram or a bus that are connected to the edge of the city center.

© *OpenStreetMap contributors*

If you are already in Estonia or in neighboring European countries, you can go to Tallinn by ferry, bus, car, or train.

Ferries go to Tallinn from Helsinki several times daily with travel durations of 2-3 hours. There are also ferries that travel between Stockholm and Tallinn every night. But, this takes about 15 hours of travel time. Many cruises also include Tallinn as one of their destinations which makes it the 3rd busiest destination for cruises in the Baltic Sea region.

If you are in a European city, you can take international buses that connect to Tallinn. Regular bus routes connect Tallinn with St. Petersburg, Vilnius, and Riga. These buses are available several times daily.

For a more convenient travel, you can also take your own car to Tallinn by driving through Russia and Latvia. You can also take your car on ferries from Stockholm and Helsinki.

Travelers from Moscow can also take an international train which connects directly to Tallinn.

Walking and Riding Bikes

Since Tallinn is a compact city, going in and around on foot won't be difficult to do. But, another option is by riding bicycles.

You can rent a bike and go around town using the city's high-quality bicycle routes. These connect many of the suburb and city's areas.

But if you are not into bikes, you can also use the city's public transport systems and taxis.

City Bike Phone: +372 511 1819

Public Transport

You can get around Central Tallinn by trams, trolleys, and buses which operate from 6 AM to 11 Pm or sometimes until 12 MN. You would need a validated ticket to ride the public transport which will be randomly inspected. You won't need to show any ticket to the driver once you board. But if you can't show a validated ticket during an inspection, you may be fined €40.

Some riders can use the transport system for free. They include children under the age of 7, adults traveling with a child younger than 3 years old, and registered Tallinn locals with an ID and a personalized Smartcard.

Tallinn Ticket System

There are several ticket types that you can purchase to use Tallinn's public transportation network.

- **Tallinn Card**

The first type is the Tallinn Card. It gives you unlimited use of the public transport for a limited period. You may also use the Tallinn Card to avail of a free sightseeing tour, free museum admissions, and discounts.

You can purchase Tallinn Cards for children (aged 0-17) and adults (aged 18 and above). They are available in 24, 48, and 72-hour durations. Purchasing an adult card will let you bring two children (7 years old and below) for free.

Tallinn Card prices range from €25-€45 for adults and €14-€23 for children. Tallinn Card Plus prices range from €36-€58 for adults and €20-€32 for children. The prices will depend on the duration of the card you will purchase.

- **Smartcard**

The Smartcard or Ühiskaart is a green, plastic card that can be used with the electronic ticket system. You will need to deposit €2 at any post office, R-Kiosk, or customer service desk of the Tallinn City Government to get a Smartcard. You will then need to load credits into the Smartcard.

Smartcard fares would range from €1.10 for a 1-hour ticket up to €23 for a 30-day ticket. The electronic system keeps track of your Smartcard use. It also charges you based on the cheapest ticket you can purchase.

How to use the Smartcard

Place your Smartcard on the orange validator by the vehicle's door. You must do this every time you ride a vehicle for ticket validation. You will see a green light after your ticket has been successfully validated. When you see a red light, it may mean that you don't have enough credits or your card is not valid.

If you are using a Smartcard for several riders, place it on the validator and you may select up to 6 riders using the arrow keys. After the number of riders has been selected, press "OK".

The validator will display the credits left on your Smartcard.

How to add more credits to the Smartcard

You may reload your Smartcard credits at the same places where the card can be bought. Adding more credits is also possible by phone or through the website https://tallinn.pilet.ee/buy.

· **QR Ticket**

QR Tickets are electronic travel tickets that use QR codes. You can use your smartphone or print out a copy of the ticket when riding the public transport.

These tickets can only be used for up to ten trips. When purchasing a QR ticket, you need to select the number of trips to determine the price. You can validate it the same way as a Smartcard.

QR Tickets can also be used to pay for several people during a single trip. You can do this the same way as you would use a Smartcard.

You can buy QR Tickets at https://tallinn.pilet.ee/buy .After paying for the ticket, an e-mail of the ticket will be sent to you or you can download it directly from the site. You can also buy them using a mobile app, Pilet.ee, which can be downloaded from the Apple App Store or the Google Play Store. Buying through the mobile app will charge you an extra €0.32.

· **Paper Tickets**

If you don't want to purchase or use a Tallinn card or a Smartcard, you can also go the traditional way – using paper tickets. Paper tickets are for single rides only. They are bought from drivers using cash when you board a public transport. Tickets costs €2 and you would need to give an exact amount. They are only valid for the vehicle you will ride on.

Taxi

For a more convenient way of traveling, you can ride taxis which are often found at taxi stands located at key intersections and in front of some hotels. You can also order a taxi through mobile apps and by phone calls.

Taxis don't have a fixed rate. The rate would depend on the taxi's operator or company. On the taxi's right rear window, you will find a yellow sticker posted with the rate. If you want to be sure, you may also ask the taxi driver for the trip's estimated cost in advance. Don't forget to ask if the price is per person or per ride.

When riding a taxi, it is important to know these basic facts:

(1)Pay the taxi driver in Euros. Some taxis may accept your payment using your bank card, but it is better to have some cash on hand.

(2)Always check if the taxi's meter is on.

(3)A taxi driver is not allowed to ask for a higher price than what is on the meter.

(4)It is illegal for taxi drivers and passengers to smoke inside the taxis.

(5)A taxi driver must always give a receipt. If the meter's printer is not working and can't provide any receipt, the driver should not be servicing in the first place. This gives you the right to decline paying the taxi fare.

If you experience any illegalities with your taxi driver, you can file a complaint to the Tallinn Municipal Police Department.

In cases where you can't find a taxi near your area, you can use your smartphone to request drivers or order taxis. Three popular taxi service mobile apps in Tallinn are Taxofon, Taxify, and Uber.

4

Top 5 Affordable Hotels

One of the essential parts of traveling is finding the perfect accommodation at the lowest price possible. You may try to get the cheapest hotel you can find, but you might risk on ruining your vacation.

So to help you get the most out of your trip, here are the top 5 hotels in Tallinn that would not break the bank.

Centennial Hotel Tallinn
Endla Str. 15, 10122 Tallinn
Phone: +372 647 4700

Location – Many tourists love staying at the Centennial Hotel for its location. It is located at the center of the city, so it is easy to get to the different tourist spots in the city. It is about 0.37 miles from the Toompea Castle and the Maiden Tower, and about 0.3 miles away from the Niguliste Museum-Concert Hall.

It is easy to get to the hotel from the airport by taxi and tram. While the bus stations are near the hotel, you would only need to walk for a few minutes to get to these stations from the hotel.

Food – Accommodations include free breakfast, and many commend the hotel's delicious breakfast and restaurant food. The breakfast has a lot of variety which appeals to tourists from different countries.

Rooms and Facilities – One of the most notable items in their hotel rooms is their comfortable beds. Their rooms also have wide screen TVs, tea and coffee commodities, and basic toiletries. Pets are not allowed in the hotel, so it is best to not bring them along.

The rooms including the bathrooms are generally spotless. Wi-Fi is free and accessible throughout the hotel. They also have a bar and lounge area, and most areas are wheelchair accessible. Their private parking space costs €15 a day.

Services – Room services are available until 2 AM and are usually quick. Many hotel guests have given great feedback for the friendly and prompt staff.

Other hotel services which you can avail of include dry cleaning, housekeeping, airport shuttles, 24-hour concierge, baggage storage, and banquet/meeting rooms. Though, some of these services have additional charges.

Prices – The room rates are reasonable given their high quality services and facilities. Their standard room average prices may range from €75 to €147.

My Apartments
Sakala 11, 10141 Tallinn
Phone: +372 507 1535

Location – My Apartments hotel is located near many tourist spots in Tallinn. It is about 5 minutes away from the Tallinn Airport by Tram #4, and 10 minutes away from the Old Town. The Estonian National Opera is just 300 meters away from the hotel, so you can easily walk going there.

Food – The hotel doesn't offer any free meals with their accommodations, but they have a cafeteria located on the building's ground floor where guests can have their breakfast. Restaurants and other places where you can buy food are just 5 minutes away on foot.

Rooms and Facilities – An apartment includes a spacious lounge and a dining and kitchen area with a stovetop, a refrigerator, and a microwave. The bathrooms have towel warmers and the floors are heated, which is perfect when you visit Tallinn during cold seasons.

Every apartment also has a washing machine, free Wi-Fi, and a TV with various international channels.

Services – According to some travelers who have tried the My Apartments, the staff in the hotel are efficient and friendly. Room cleaning service is done every 3 days, but the staff takes out the garbage from the apartment daily.

Prices – Standard room average prices range from €56 up to €91. Their rates are relatively lower compared to other hotels.

Paivilla Boutique Hotel
5 Laine, Kristiine, 11314 Tallinn
Phone: +372 501 1499

Location – The landmarks nearest the Paivilla Boutique Hotel are the A. Le Coq Arina and the Alexela Concert Hall. It is also near the historical Toompea Castle.

It only takes a few minutes to reach the hotel from the airport. You can easily reach the city center by bus since there is a bus station 5 minutes away from the hotel on foot.

Food – Accommodations include a large breakfast with a fair amount of choices.

Rooms and Facilities – The hotel is highly rated for its comfortable beds, decently decorated rooms, and free parking. You can use their outdoor picnic areas and barbeque facilities. There is also a garden where you can lounge and relax.

They have a lot of enjoyable and relaxing facilities including a sauna (additional fees will be charged), a playground and other recreational activities for children, a library, and a game room. The hotel allows pets upon request and they also offer free Wi-Fi.

Services – The front desk is available 24 hours and many guests find the staff to be friendly and accommodating. If you are checking in with a pet you may request for pet bowls. You can also utilize the hotels shared lounge and TV area.

Prices – Standard room prices may range from €59 to €92 a night.

Tallinn Apartment Hotel
Väike-Ameerika 24 (24/1), 10129 Tallinn
Phone: +372 56 957 758

Location – This hotel is at the center of Tallinn. It is near the Old Town, A. Le Coq Arena, Kristiine Shopping Centre, St. Charles' Church, and the Freedom Square.

The Tallinn Apartment Hotel is located about a mile away from the Tallinn Train Station and about a mile and a half away from the Tallinn International Bus Station.

Food – They don't serve any meals with your accommodation, but there is Café Kohalik that is near the hotel if you want to eat good food around a great atmosphere.

Rooms and Facilities – The hotel only has a total of 10 available apartments that you can rent, so it is best to reserve early. All rooms have 1 bedroom, but the apartments have various sizes which can cater from 2 to 6 people.

Their apartments have free Wi-Fi, air conditioned rooms (heating is also available during cold seasons), a living room with a flat screen TV, and a kitchen with complete equipment. You can lounge in their closed backyard while the children can spend time at the playground.

Guests can only smoke at a designated area because they prohibit smoking in all other areas in the hotel. If you are bringing a car, you can park for free at their secured parking area. They also provide an airport shuttle for an additional charge. Pets are not allowed in this hotel.

Services – Their staff is friendly, quick, and accommodating. But, there are additional charges if you want to avail of their daily house-keeping service.

Prices – The average price for their standard rooms range from €74 to €169.

Tallinn City Apartments Old Town Suites
Vana-Posti, 10146 Tallinn
Phone: +372 525 5321

Location – The Tallinn City Apartments Old Town Suites is located in Old Town. It is near many historical sites like the Toompea Castle, the War of Independence Victory Column, and the Kiek in de Kok.

It is also at the center of various shopping centers, grocery stores, restaurants, and night life establishments.

Food – There are not any food served at the hotel, but there are tons of restaurants nearby with a variety of food choices.

Rooms and Facilities – According to many guests, the rooms are clean, comfortable, and well-maintained. They are also soundproof and air conditioned. But, bathrooms may be too small for some. Accommodations come with free Wi-Fi.

This is not a place for smokers because all rooms and spaces are non-smoking areas. The parking spaces are well-secured, but they cost €10 a day. The hotel also has a sauna where you can relax especially during cold seasons.

Services – The staff is helpful, efficient, and accommodating. They offer cleaning and laundry services. Other services include baggage storage and express check-ins and check-outs.

Prices – Their prices may vary from different apartment sizes, but you will be asked for a damage deposit of €200 upon arrival. You may reimburse the deposit when you check-out after an inspection of your apartment has been done.

Other Budget Hotels You May Consider

Hotel St. Barbara
+372 640 0040

Park Inn by Radisson Central Tallinn
+372 633 9800

5

Top 5 Restaurants

It may be difficult to choose from the many restaurants Tallinn has to offer. But, you can expect that most, if not all, restaurants will serve you only the best quality foods and dishes.

Restaurants in Tallinn offer food inspired by diverse cuisine. There are restaurants which offer authentic Estonian food, while some would be a fusion of different international cuisines. There are also restaurants which serve food influenced by the city's former rulers, the Soviet Union.

If you are staying for a short time in Tallinn and could not go to all the restaurants in the city, take a look at this list of the top 5 restaurants in Tallinn.

NOA
Ranna tee 3, 12111 Tallinn
Phone:+372 508 0589

You can enjoy a stunning view of the Tallinn Bay, great wine, and amazing international cuisine at NOA. When it opened in 2014, many locals and tourists immediately loved the restaurant's food and modern design.

It is a low-level establishment with tables and seats placed on different levels, so every customer has a view of the Tallinn Bay and the Old Town. With their stunning and modern design, it is no surprise that this restaurant has won several awards.

At the "Chef's Hall", you can have a seven or five-course meal consisting of inventive and delicious dishes. Both vegan and non-vegan customers have a variety of dishes to choose from.

NOA can become quite busy and packed with customers especially during seasons where there are a lot of tourists in Tallinn. It may be best to contact the restaurant in advance to reserve a table.

JUUR
Valukoja 10, 11415 Tallinn
Phone:+372 607 0705

JUUR is located in Ülemiste City. It is a restaurant that was build from an old factory. They offer a Nordic cuisine fine dining experience with the use of organic ingredients which are locally-sourced. You can also enjoy a variety of Estonian drinks like craft beers and wines.

Their menu highlights the use of molecular gastronomy to create unique dishes. You can choose from their main menu, set menu, and business lunch menu.

The main menu consists of a fair selection of à la carte appetizers, entrées, and desserts. They also have salty and sweet snacks. Their set menu has five- to seven-course options. Their business lunch menu varies on the day you will be dining with them and it is only available from Monday to Friday.

Ö
Mere Puiestee 6e, 10111 Tallinn
Phone:+372 661 6150

Despite belonging to the top restaurants in Tallinn, Ö has one of the lowest profiles. It is an Estonian restaurant which offers authentic Northern cuisine.

The restaurant's head chefs work with local farmers and producers where they get the best local raw ingredients from the north. The chefs and kitchen staff go on harvesting trips which let them create distinctly flavored dishes. The chefs personally pick out and collect the raw ingredients, so you can be sure that you will be served only the best Tallinn has to offer.

Their menu has a range of deconstructed Estonian classic dishes which take tourists and locals on a gastronomical adventure to the past. They also apply Estonian cooking methods with their dishes.

Leib Resto ja Aed (Restaurant Leib)
Uus 31, 10111 Tallinn
Phone: +372 611 9026

Restaurant Leib (Estonian word for "bread") is famous for their handmade bread and dishes that highlight the freshness and simplicity of locally collected ingredients.

It is considered one of the hidden gems of Tallinn in the Old Town. Tourists and locals love the charming atmosphere of the restaurant with its beautiful terrace and garden.

Leib is run by a sommelier and a chef who will make sure that you are served with dishes that match perfectly with their beers and wines. Their prices are reasonable and more affordable compared to other fine dining restaurants in the city.

Salt
Vase 14, 10125 Tallinn
Phone:+372 518 8510

Salt is located in the residential area of Kadriorg. It is another restaurant hidden from the bustling commercial areas of Tallinn. Despite having a short menu, many customers have expressed their delight with Salt's unique and great-tasting dishes.

They offer progressive food inspired by international cuisines. You will be served food from an open kitchen. So if you are looking for a cozy restaurant, extra friendly service, and a wine selection you wouldn't find elsewhere, then Salt is the place for you.

Other Restaurants You May Want to Visit

Alexander Chef's Table
Phone: +372 60 22 222

Art Priori
Phone:+372 600 33 53

Ribe
Phone:+372 6140085

6

Best Famous Landmarks

Tallinn, being a UNESCO Heritage Site, is filled with historical land-marks and places which reflect Estonia's culture.

The whole city itself looks like it has been preserved from the medieval times. But, there are a number of modern structures and establishments that have been built to boost the city's tourism.

If you have no idea about the famous spots in Tallinn, here is a list of the best landmarks in the city that you must see especially on your first visit.

Raekoja Plats (Town Hall Square)

The Raekoja Plats or the Town Hall Square is located at the center of the Old Town. It is beside the Tallinn Town Hall. It is packed with many stalls, souvenir shops, bars, and restaurants.

In the past, it was a meeting and market place for locals and traders. There was also one execution in this area due to a disagreement over an omelet.

Today, the square is a popular venue for concerts, medieval-themed markets, and handicraft fairs.

During winter, you can enjoy shopping at their Christmas Market and viewing the Christmas tree that's placed at the Raekoja Plats which has been the city's tradition since 1441. In spring, be amazed with the medieval-style carnival called the Old Town Days festival.

There are also medieval festivals during summer. You will also find a lot of outdoor cafes, fairs, and concerts in this season.

Tallinn Old Town

Besides the Town Hall Square and the Tallinn Town Hall, you will also find other historical and modern sites in Tallinn Old Town.

The Old Town consists of the upper town (also known as Toompea) and the lower town. In the past, gates separated these two towns. But now, you will be able to see a beautiful skyline formed between them.

Walking through the Old Town may be one of the best activities to do when you are in Tallinn. Many tourists admire the beauty of its colorful buildings and cobblestone streets.

You can find restaurants almost everywhere in the Old Town. If you want to dine in a more peaceful restaurant with fewer tourists, you may want to walk farther away from the commercial area center.

Toompea Hill

One of the most popular sights you must not miss when you are in the Old Town is Toompea Hill. Many hotels are located near the Toompea Hill, so it is easy to walk to this beautiful and historic landmark.

According to legend, the Toompea Hill is the Estonian King Kalev's burial mold which makes it a special part of Estonia's culture.

Many beautiful and important buildings were built on the hill including the Toompea Castle, Gothic Toomkirk, and the Alexander Nevsky Cathedral. All of these wonderful structures were built close with each other, so it is quite easy to visit them on foot.

Once you are on the Toompea Hill, you will be able to see an amazing view of the entire city of Tallinn.

Kohtuotsa Viewing Point

The Kohtuotsa is one of the two viewing points on the Toompea Hill. It is located on the northern side of the hill which provides a breathtaking view of the Old Town.

Kohtuotsa Platform

This viewing platform is spacious enough for tourists who want to view and take pictures of the city's medieval neighborhood. Tallinn's ancient spires and modern towers are also clearly visible from Kohtuotsa.

In summer, you can relax at a pop-up outdoor café and join the dance in the evenings.

Kadriorg Palace

Considered as the grandest park and palace design example of Estonian architecture, the Kadriorg is definitely a must-see landmark. It was originally used as a royal summer residence.

The palace is well preserved by the government, so you can see all the beautiful architectural details which resemble Italian palaces during the time it was built.

Kadriorg Palace

The palace's façade have 2 levels at the back and 3 levels at the front. You will find a winter garden and a banquet hall at the back façade which were added in 1933 or 1934.

Today, the Estonian Art Museum uses the palace for their foreign art collection.

Other Famous Landmarks You Must Visit

Patkuli Viewing Platform
Rahukohtu, 10130

Phone:+372 645 7777

Town Hall Pharmacy
Raekoja plats 11
Phone:+372 631 4860

Town Wall
Väike-Kloostri 1

Viru Gates

Viru gates

St. Catherine's Passage

Pikk Tanav (Long Street)

St. Catherine's Passage

7

Best Museums

Tallinn is also home to many museums. There are specialty museums which focus on specific historical and cultural aspects of the city.

Museums in Tallinn offer many activities and programs which you will enjoy. All the museums are well-curated and preserved.

To know more about the museums that may interest you, here are the details of the best museums in Tallinn.

Tallinn Museum of Orders of Knighthood
Kuninga 3, Old Town, 10146 Tallinn

Phaleristics scholars and hobbyists would truly enjoy visiting the Tallinn Museum of Orders of Knighthood. It features several historical jewelries and designs from the Orders of the Garter to the Legion of Honour.

You will learn much about the history of the Orders of Chivalry through various stars, badges, and collars displayed in the museum which reflect exquisite craftsmanship.

Many pieces in their collection belonged to princes, princesses, emperors, military commanders, politicians, and presidents. But, the highlight pieces in the museum include Ethiopian Emperor Haile Selassie's insignia and Emperor of Russia Peter the Great's Order of the White Eagle among all others.

They have a souvenir shop in the museum where you can buy imitations of different decorative ornaments, history books, and collective stamps.

Kumu Art Museum
A. Weizenbergi 34, 10127 Tallinn

The Kumu Art Museum is by far the most advanced and the largest art museum in Estonia. Here, you will find a vast collection of Estonian artwork starting from the 18th century until 1991.

The art museum opened in 2006 and has become a multi-purpose structure. At Kumu, you will find the art conservation-restoration department, a modern art gallery, an educational center, an auditorium, a library, and several art exhibitions. Art exhibitions include permanent ones by Kumu and variable ones which feature contemporary and international arts.

The Kumu Art Museum's complex is also considered a contemporary architectural masterpiece. This limestone and copper structure's sharp and curved edges make this museum a marvelous work of art.

Seaplane Harbour
Vesilennuki 6, 10415 Tallinn

If you are visiting Tallinn with your family, you would probably enjoy the Seaplane Harbour (Estonian Maritime Museum).

It features about 200 unique and historical items including, the submarine Lembit, the seaplane Short 184, the remains of some of the oldest Estonian ships, and the 100-year old icebreaker Suur Tõll.

There are also many activities to do at Seaplane Harbour. Besides the interactive exhibitions, there are also two cinemas, simulators, a children's corner, an aquarium, an outdoor playground, the famous café MARU, and a souvenir shop. The museum also has a photo booth where you can be in a navy uniform.

Estonian Health Care Museum
Lai 30, 10133 Tallinn

While at the Tallinn Old Town, you must visit the Estonian Health Care Museum. Opened in 1924, the museum is home to a permanent health care and anatomy exhibition.

The exhibition is called "About Your Body, Openly and Honestly" where you can learn all about the human body and ancient medicine. You can also learn about human evolution, disease diagnostics, and healthy eating.

Children, as well as adults, will enjoy the interactive mechanical and electronic exhibits. You will also find their collection of items that reflect the medical heritage of Estonia.

Besides fun and educational exhibits, the museum also has facilities and rooms for birthday parties and other special events.

Estonian Open Air Museum
Vabaõhumuuseumi tee 12, 13521 Tallinn

To understand more about village life in Estonia, you should visit the Estonian Open Air Museum. The museum features recreated rural villages from the 18th to 20th centuries.

You can find several farm structures, a village school, a wooden chapel, and historic windmills in the forest park. The museum's staff is dressed in period costumes while they demonstrate the lives and work of people in the past.

The Estonian Open Air Museum is located by the Rocca al Mare seaside area.

After touring around the museum, you can go on a picnic with your family and friends. You can also enjoy their themed fairs with songs, dances, and games. You can purchase handicrafts from their souvenir shop and eat traditional foods at the village tavern.

Other Museums You May Want to Visit

Telliskivi Loomelinnak
CPQH+WH Tallinn, Harju County
Phone: +372 520 4791

Niguliste Museum

CPPV+94 Tallinn, Harju County

Phone:+372 631 4330

Tallinna Linnamuuseum

CPQX+F7 Tallinn, Harju County

Phone:+372 615 5180

Estonian Maritime Museum

CPVX+2Q Tallinn, Harju County

Phone:+372 641 1408

KGB Museum

CQP3+JW Tallinn, Harju County

Phone:+372 680 9300

Vabamu Museum of Occupations and Freedom

CPMQ+2Q Tallinn, Harju County

Phone: +372 668 0250

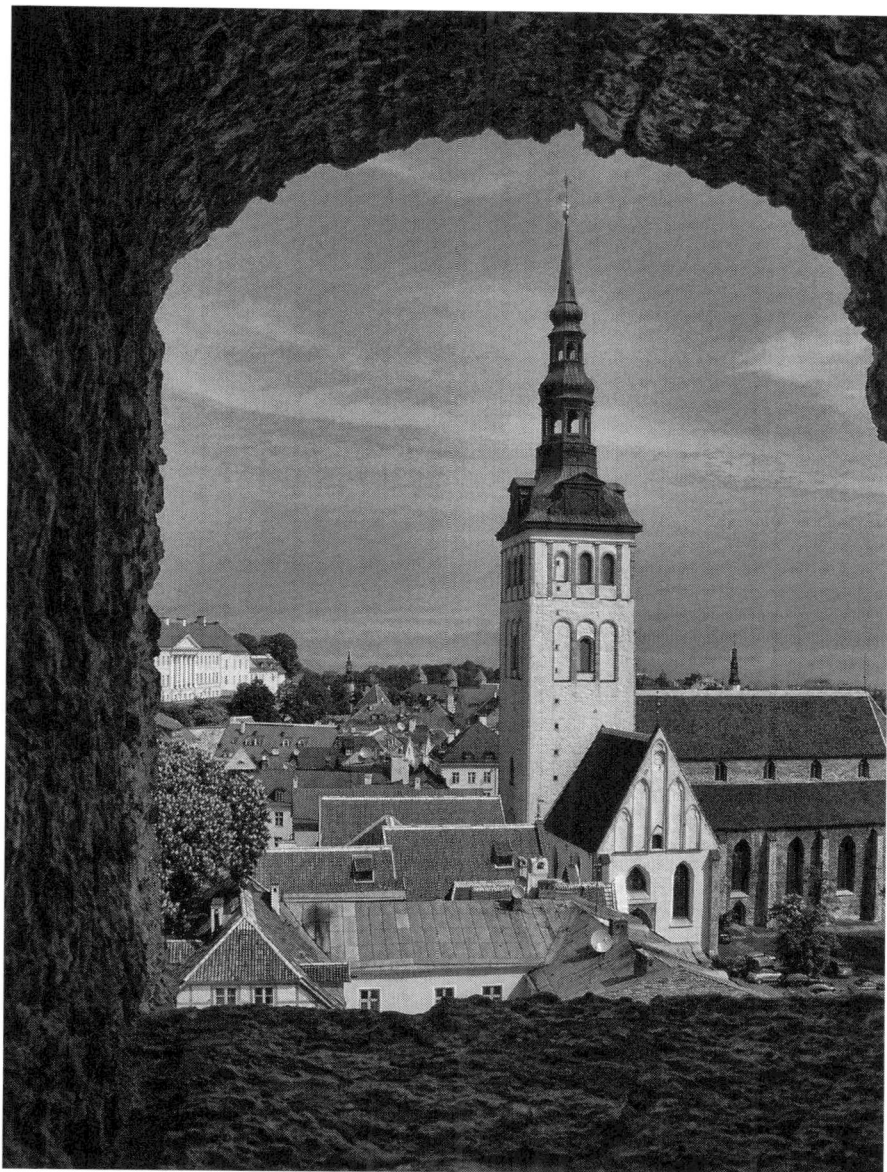

8

Best Art Galleries

Art lovers would want to visit Tallinn's art galleries which feature historical and contemporary art of local artists in Tallinn.

Many art galleries hold exhibitions all-year-round. So no matter what time of the year you visit, you will be able to see an art exhibit in Tallinn.

Here are some of the best art galleries in Tallinn that you must visit.

Tallinn Art Hall & Galleries
Vabaduse väljak 6 | Vabaduse väljak 8| Harju 13, 10146 Tallinn

There are about three exhibit halls that you shouldn't miss when you are in Tallinn – the Art Hall Gallery (Vabaduse väljak 6), the Tallinn Art Hall (Vabaduse väljak 8), and the Tallinn City Gallery (Harju 13).

These art exhibit halls feature amazing contemporary art programs which help artists create different artworks and exhibits. The galleries can host up to 24 exhibits yearly, so you will always have something to see no matter what time of the year you visit.

They also host exhibits for international artists. The galleries feature tours, concerts, and educational programs for children among many other events.

Design & Architecture Gallery

Pärnu mnt 6, 10148 Tallinn

The Design & Architecture Gallery in Tallinn holds exhibits which feature Estonian architecture and design. The exhibits are non-profit and are sponsored by different artists.

They also hold exhibits for international art and design projects. They can be unpredictable because they sometimes hold a pop-up restaurant at festivals or they may host exhibits by Gingerbread Mania.

Draakoni Gallery

Pikk 18, 10133 Tallinn

Established in April 1983, the Draakoni Gallery focused on hosting exhibits of artworks by the Graphic Artists Society members in their first few years.

The gallery then became an outlet for selling graphic art, paintings, and applied arts. They only resumed hosting art exhibits in 2003. The exhibits feature works by Estonian and international artists. They also have joined art education programs and continued selling contemporary Estonian paintings, photography, and graphic arts.

You can easily find the Draakoni Gallery in the Art Nouveau structure in the Old Town where you will see dragons in the gallery's façade.

Haus Gallery
Uus 17, 10123 Tallinn

The Haus Gallery is a young gallery which only started in 1997. They were once located in Kadriorg, but they relocated to Uus St. in the Old Town in 2000.

They have two exhibition halls which focus on old and contemporary Estonian art. The exhibits are changed on a monthly basis. They also hold art auctions and other services such as appraisals.

If you would like to buy Estonian artwork, you can participate in the Haus Gallery's auctions. They focus on paintings compiled with the help of foreign and local collectors, and art experts and historians.

Navitrolla Gallery
Sulevimägi 1, 10123 Tallinn

The Navitrolla Gallery is home to Heiki Trolla's (Navitrolla) art masterpieces. Being a well-known Estonian artist, Navitrolla created a gallery for his artworks.

His surrealist art is popular locally and internationally, so you may want to spend some of your extra cash to purchase one of his oil paintings or other graphics.

Some of Navitrolla's works may be available in other countries, but his oil paintings can only be purchased in his gallery.

9

Best Coffee Shops

You must not leave Tallinn without having at least a cup of their locally-grown coffee.

There are many coffee shops in Tallinn that serve coffee that had been roasted and grown locally. Some even serve coffee that you can only get in Tallinn.

For an amazing breakfast to start your day in the city, visit these coffee shops which are considered some of the best Tallinn has to offer.

Gourmet Coffee
L. Koidula 13A, Kadriorg | Pärnu maantee 15, City Center | Valuoja 10, Ülemiste

Gourmet Coffee can be found in three different locations – the Tallinn City Center, Kadriorg, and Ülemiste.

They only use high-quality roasted coffee from Coffee People, a popular roaster in Estonia. Gourmet Coffee's baristas are considered some of the best baristas in Estonia. Just request any kind of coffee you want, and they will create it for you.

Besides great-tasting coffee, they also serve healthy meals and snacks, pastries, and Emeyu tea. To complete your Tallinn experience, you may also avail of their barista training and learn to whip up some delicious coffee.

RØST Bakery & Café
Rotermanni tänav 14, 10111 Tallinn

RØST (pronounced as röst) is a small Scandinavian-influenced bakery located in Tallinn. They take pride in their sourdough breads where they use natural leavening agents. They also make sandwiches and pastries.

To let visitors enjoy their bread even more, they offer coffee using beans from the best Estonian and foreign micro-roasteries.

The only downside is that they have a small dining space. Since this bakery and café is famous with locals and tourists, it is often crowded.

Epic Coffee
Müürivahe 36, 10140 Tallinn

Their name says it all – Epic Coffee serves epic-tasting coffee. They serve various caffeinated drinks such as matcha latte and decaf cappuccino.

Whether hot or cold, you can request just about any coffee you like. They also serve teas and a selection of savory and sweet snacks.

The café is cozy and simple. Many visitors consider it a perfect place to get breakfast.

The Living Room Café
Pärnu mnt 9, 10141 Tallinn

The Living Room Café is run by student volunteers who keep the prices reasonable. The design and seating give the café a cozy atmosphere that will make you stay for hours. The perfect time to visit the café is in the evening and on weekends where they have open-mic events and live music.

Their specialty coffee is made from hand-roasted beans which they roast in-house weekly. They also use different brewing methods depending on the type of coffee you order. You can also order delicious foods which are all freshly made that will match your coffee.

Grenka Café
Pärnu maantee 76, 10131 Tallinn

If you don't like fancy and complicated dishes, then Grenka Café is the place for you. They serve simple and healthy food that would remind you of home.

This Grenka is recognized by the Flavours of Estonia and the White Guide as a restaurant that you must visit when you are in Tallinn. Many locals and tourists visit this Belarusian restaurant for their pies and grenkas.

But another highlight of this place is their coffee. They have an assortment of coffee and tea choices. They are not as fancy as other café's, but you will be served with high-quality coffee which is perfect for breakfast.

Other Coffee Shops You May Want to Visit

Babulja Kohvik-Kokteilibaar
CPPX+9R Tallinn, Harju County

Maiasmokk Cafe
Pikk 16, 10123 Tallinn

10

Top 5 Bars

For beer and wine drinkers, Tallinn also has plenty of bars and local pubs that you can visit. There are popular beer brands that are brewed in Tallinn. Some pubs also brew homemade beer in-house. Beer is also cheaper in Tallinn compared to neighboring cities and countries.

Get in touch with the locals over a pint of beer at these top bars in Tallinn.

Valli Baar
Müürivahe 14, 10146 Tallinn

For a one of a kind experience, don't forget to visit Valli Baar. Once you are inside, you will feel as if you had traveled back to the 70s. In fact, Valli Baar is protected as a cultural heritage structure.

You may have a hard time finding a seat in this small bar since it is famous with both tourists and locals.

If you truly want your Tallinn vacation to be memorable, you can try their iconic Millimallikas (Estonian word for jellyfish). It is a strong cocktail which is a blend of tequila, Sambucca, and Tabasco sauce.

Shvips
Telliskivi 51i, 10412 Tallinn

Wine aficionados should never forget to visit Shvips. Located in Tallinn's Telliskivi district, this bar houses over 200 different kinds of wines.
Enjoy your wine in an eccentric and comfortable atmosphere.

Their snack selection is also quite special. Choose from different high-quality deli meats, cheeses, and olives which they get from Estonia, the Netherlands, and Italy. You will also be served with some grilled ciabatta.

Kolu Tavern
Vabaõhumuuseumi tee 12, 13521 Tallinn

If you visit the Estonian Open Air Museum, you should not skip going inside the Kolu Tavern (also called Kolu Inn).

It was once located in a village in 1840. Then in 1968, it was transferred to the museum. After being reconstructed in 1969 to 1973, the tavern was able to operate again in 1993.

They serve Estonian traditional food in an old-fashioned dining experience. You can also join the folk dance performances at night.

You can also avail of their Estonian food tasting packages where you will be served different kinds of ciders, wines, and beers which are all made in-house.

Speakeasy by Põhjala

Kopli 4, 10412 Tallinn

Speakeasy by Põhjala is a hidden hipster bar located in Kalamaja area. They serve an impressive selection of high-quality beer from the Põhjala brewery. A Põhjala beer is considered one of the most famous beers in Estonia.

The bar is quite small, but you can use their courtyard's terrace which is large enough to accommodate many locals and tourists.

Woodstock
Tatari 6, 10141 Tallinn

Being one of the few last standing rock bars in Tallinn, you must visit Woodstock. But be warned, this place is not for the faint of heart because people here can get really crazy.

The bar is spacious with high ceilings. You will see memorabilia of Estonian rock history and Estonia's football team on the walls. Enjoy affordable drinks while listening to some 60's and 70's music.

You can also watch rock gigs at the basement of the bar. There are also football and pool tables.

Other Bars You May Want to Visit

Hr. Mauruse Pub
Estonia pst 8

11

Top 5 Nightclubs

The party scene is also the reason for many tourists to visit Tallinn. There are numerous nightclubs where you can experience amazing parties, programs, and events.

You can also find eccentric nightclubs that you won't find anywhere else in the world.

Look into these top 5 nightclubs in Tallinn for a night you won't forget.

Club Hollywood
Vana-Posti 8, 10146 Tallinn

Club Hollywood is one of Tallinn's most popular nightclubs. It is always packed with locals and tourists almost all-year-round. It is located in the heart of Old Town.

They have top-of-the-line equipment and enough room for 1,500 people. There is also a VIP bar which is separated from the larger VIP area with tables.

The club's bartenders have won numerous awards, so you can be sure that you will get the best service. But, Club Hollywood is most proud of their DJs. Some of the best DJs in Estonia and in other countries perform in this club.

They also organize different popular events including Dance of Colors, Grind, and Ladies Nights (every Wednesday).

Rock Club Tapper
Pärnu maantee 158, 11317 Tallinn

First opened in 2008, Rock Club Tapper is an important venue is Estonia's rock scene. The club was specially made to host rock concerts and it can house up to 600 people.

You can watch performances from metal, hard rock, and thrash bands that often come from Latvia and Finland. Some gigs are free, since they make money with their bar. But, international and bigger gigs are not free.

You can also visit the club for drinks, meals, and pool games when there are no concerts happening.

Klubi Teater
Vabaduse väljak 5, 10141 Tallinn

Klubi Teater (Club Teater) is a young club with 1930's-inspired décor. They have combined contemporary and historical glamour designs to create an interesting atmosphere for their guests.

Teater offers diverse entertainment performances and programs. Popular artists such as bands, singers, and DJs perform during themed events and are accompanied by dancers. You will also be served by professional trained staff.

Culture Club Kelm
Vene 33, 10123 Tallinn

The Culture Club Kelm is widely popular especially for young culture enthusiasts.

The club is often filled with young people who take part in their events which are held 4-5 nights weekly. Some events include movie viewing, game nights, art shows, and even workshops. Live bands and DJs perform at the Kelm weekly.

The Kelm was started by young creative people for the younger crowd. But, anybody is welcome in the club.

Privé
Harju 6, 10130 Tallinn

Club Privé is located beside the Freedom Square which became quickly popular among music lovers, social elites, and fashion-inclined people.

They can be a bit pricey and you may need to dress up to get inside, but you should not miss it. You will enjoy dancing to urban music from local and international DJs and live bands.

They also host various events throughout the year.

Other Nightclubs You May Want to Visit

Venus
CQP3+R2 Tallinn
+372 551 9999

Vabank
CPMV+QG Tallinn
+372 660 5299

12

Things You Can Only Do In Tallinn

Tallinn Towers

Go on a Tallinn Guided Walk Tour

To know more about Estonia, going on a walk tour that may last for 2-5 hours is one of the activities that you must include in your travel itinerary. You will be toured around by a guide around Tallinn's historical sites.

The tours would probably take you around lower town before going to upper town. There are many local guides who can tour you around the most famous sights in the city.

You might first go to the Pikk Street, the Dominican monastery, craftsmen guilds, and merchant homes in lower town.

In upper town, you will find the Lutheran St. Mary's Cathedral and Russian Orthodox Alexander Nevsky Cathedral. Beside these cathedrals is the castle of the Parliament of Estonia. Then, you may head out to the two famous viewing points to experience an amazing view of the city.

Some walk tours are free, but you can also join paid walk tours. Price ranges of guided walk tours vary on the length, the places, and inclusions of the tour.

Parliament of Estonia

Go on a Tallinn Food Tour

You can go in a food tour around Tallinn to understand more about Estonia's food and culture.

There are tons of restaurants, pubs, and cafés with outdoor seating, so you can be sure that you will be accommodated despite the large number of tourists and locals.

It will be difficult to know where to go if it is your first time in Tallinn. It is best to hire a local tour guide to get you to the best food spots in town.

You must not miss out the authentic food, liquor, and coffee which you can only find in Estonia.

If a food tour is not your thing, you can go to different restaurants and café's during different times of the day while you are in Tallinn.

Wear Costumes and Have Photos of You Taken

There are some photography studios which offer packages where you can wear realistic Medieval Age costumes in a historical building setting. It is a great way of preserving your memories of traveling to Tallinn.

Some museums like the Seaplane Harbour also offer photography services where you can wear navy uniform costumes.

Go on a Tallinn Bike Tour

Another way of touring Tallinn is by bike. It is a faster way of going in and around the city compared to walk tours. Some paid bike tours include bike rental fees.

The city also has reliable and safe bike routes, so you can always feel safe when riding a bike.

Discover the Abandoned Places in Tallinn

Steer away from the most visited and commercial tourist spots in Tallinn and go on a tour to its abandoned and historical places. Here are some of the most notable abandoned spots in Tallinn:

Riisipere Mansion – a huge abandoned manor built in 1818–1821. It is located in Vilumäe, Harju County.

Linnahall – an old amphitheater which once catered to about 5,000 people. It was built for the Moscow Olympics in 1980.
Address: CQW3+JC Tallinn, Harju County
Phone: +372 641 2250

Volta Factory – an electrical generator plant which was abandoned many years ago.
Address:CPXG+H5 Tallinn, Harju County
Phone:+372 612 0600

Patarei Prison – a Soviet prison which was also a sea fortress.

Address: FP2R+2X Tallinn, Harju County,

Kopli Lines – once used as a communal housing of the Russo-Baltic factory workers that is now abandoned.

Viivikonna – the most famous ghost town in Estonia where about 90 residents remain.

Ungru manor – an unfinished mansion with an interesting legend.
Riisipere manor – an abandoned orphanage where many claimed it to be haunted.

These sites are really old structures that can be quite dangerous. It is best to get an experienced guide to get you around these places safely.

Visit Pirita

Pirita is considered the Malibu of Estonia. You can do many activities in Pirita like sightseeing from the Tallinn TV Tower and relaxing by the beach.

There are also museums in Pirita where you can learn about Estonian history – the Estonian Film Museum and the Maarjamäe Palace and Stables.

You can also find the Metsakalmistu or the Forest Cemetery in Pirita. Many famous Estonians like artists, heroes, and politicians were buried in the cemetery.

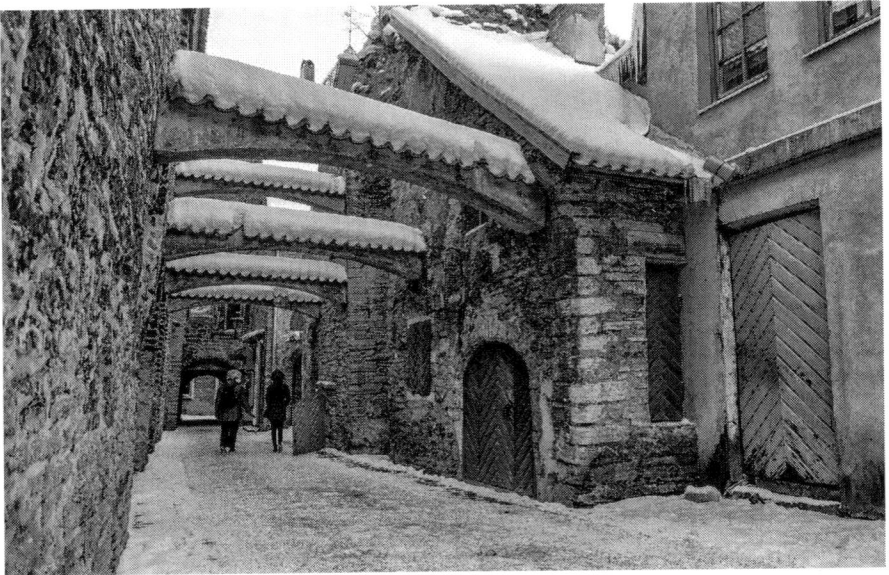

13

Traveling Safely in Tallinn

Because of the large tourist traffic that goes in and out of Tallinn, the government do everything they can to make sure that travelers are safe in the city. But like any other place in the world, you must still take extra precautions.

Wear the Right Kind of Clothing

Before going to Tallinn, be aware of the weather in the city. Make sure to bring the right kind of clothes depending on the season and weather to avoid getting ill during your trip.

If you are planning to go on walk tours, leave your high heels and sandals behind. The city's streets are mostly made out of cobblestone which can be rough and uneven. It will be better to wear and bring comfortable footwear that can support your feet well. In addition to this, bringing a stroller for an infant is not advisable. You should bring a carrier instead.

Be Vigilant Against Scammers, Thieves, and Pickpockets

Since Tallinn is often packed with tourists, it is no wonder that there are countless of pickpockets and thieves roaming the streets. They often target tourists' cash, cameras, credit cards, and anything that they can get their hands on.

Keep in mind that you won't be able to identify a pickpocket from a crowd. They can be children, old people, and even a professional-looking man or woman. They may also work in groups that execute scams or they can just quickly snatch your belongings and run away. You can report such incidences to the police, but it is less likely that they will get caught.

To avoid this, it is better to take precautions. Keep your bags secured and close to you at all times. Leave valuables that you won't really need at home. Avoid wearing anything fancy like jewelry. Be mindful of the people around you and your surroundings.

Avoid Local Ethnic Tensions

Almost all of Tallinn's population consists of ethnic Russians. Many of them may not speak Estonian and they often celebrate Russian holidays. Because of this, tension often sparks between Estonian and Russian locals. It is best to avoid these tensions. When you see some locals arguing, make your escape quickly.

Avoid Night Spots in Tallinn if Possible

If you are not going to Tallinn to drink and party, it is best to avoid the nightclubs. People from neighboring countries and cities often come to Estonia for their cheap alcoholic beverages. There are more people on the weekends where events and programs often occur.

Expect to encounter a lot of drunken people when you go to their night spots. Avoid these kinds of people, or just simply stay away from the night spots if you want to avoid trouble.

Emergency Number: 112

14

3-Day Tallinn Travel Itinerary

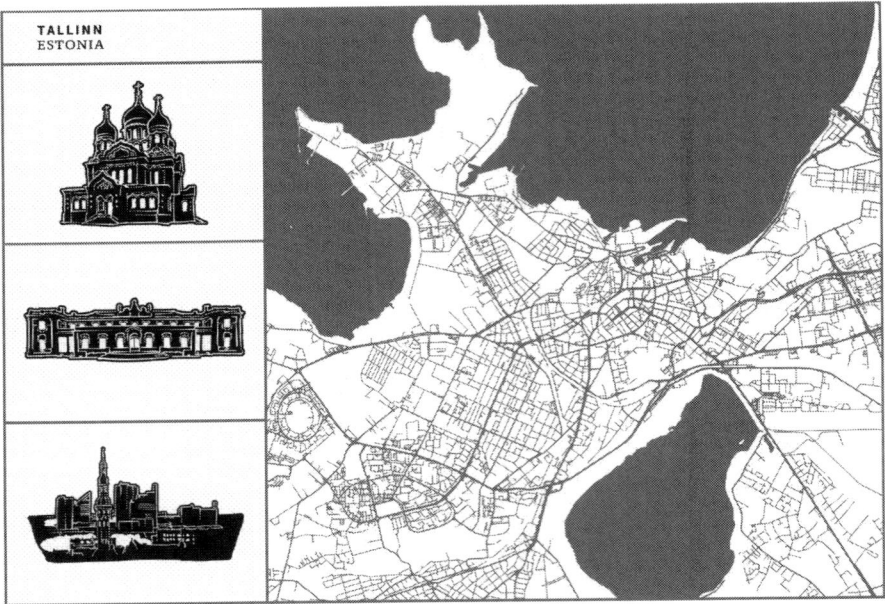

Day 1

You might still be tired from your flight if you come from a far country, so you can start your Tallinn travel with light activities.

Go on 2-3 hour walk tours in the Old Town. Most hotels that you can book are in the center of the city, so it will be easy to go on walk tours on your first day.

Start from the tower on Raekoja Plats (Town Hall Square) to get an entire view of the Old Town.

Explore the streets of the Old Town to find different shops, churches, and courtyards.

Rest at any café in the Old Town which mostly serves locally-grown and roasted coffee. If you have wandered off to Vene St., drop by Chocolaterie Pierre to try amazing Estonian chocolate.

At night have dinner in one of the many amazing restaurants in Tallinn.

If you still got some energy left in you, drop by at some local pubs that offer locally-made beers or wines to end your first day in Tallinn.

Day 2

After getting a good night's sleep, get ready to tour farther away from the heart of the city for some fun activities.

For first time travelers, head to the Kadriorg district to visit the Kumu Art Museum. If you have already been to Kumu, there are also other museums, art galleries, and other historical sites you can visit (see the Top 5 lists of places in Tallinn for ideas).

After a tour in the museum, enjoy a stroll in the peaceful Kadriorg Park. It is filled with pathways and café's where you can take a break.

Visit the Kadriorg Palace which features a collection of German, Italian, and Dutch Art.

To end Day 2 of your trip, you can either choose to relax in your hotel's sauna (which most hotels have) or you can party in one of Tallinn's amazing nightclubs.

Day 3

For your last day in Tallinn, learn more about the city's culture and history or simply enjoy at the beach and marvel at the sunset.

Head on over to Rocca al Mare district and tour around the Open Air Museum. If you want to be closer to nature, you can also try visiting the Botanical Gardens in Pirita.

Both Pirita and Rocca al Mare have restaurants and cafés you can visit to have meals and rest.

If you choose to visit Pirita, you may go for a swim at the beach, do fun activities at their adventure park, or rent a boat for a fun Pirita River adventure.

Pirita River

You may want to skip the nightclubs and pubs on your last day. Instead, finish your trip with a nice authentic Estonian meal.

This itinerary is for the best seasons in Tallinn. If you are planning on going during the winter, you may need a different itinerary since there are lots of great activities in winter.

Here are some activities to do in Tallinn during winter.

Visit the Christmas Market in Old Town

Every European trip would not be complete without a visit to a Christmas Market, and Tallinn has one. The Old Town is packed with huts and stalls selling handmade products and traditional food. You can also see various performances on weekends in this area.

View the city from the Town Hall Tower

Many people may want to see an amazing view of the city during spring or summer, but the view during winter is quite breathtaking. You will be able to see the city covered in white snow, so don't forget to take your camera with you.

Do winter activities

There are many spots in Tallinn where you can go skiing, ice skating, ice fishing, and even sledging. You can also meet adorable huskies. If you are feeling adventurous, why not try taking a dip in an ice hole?

Phone: +372 507 0317 (Play Tallinn)

Visit the frozen waterfalls

See how dropping temperatures stop time by visiting the waterfalls of Keila-Joa and Jägala. The sight of the beautiful, frozen solid waterfalls will definitely be etched into your memories forever.

Experience Saunas the Estonian Way

Estonians consider saunas as a means of socializing and relaxing with family and friends. A tradition Estonians do during winter is dipping in a cold lake or rolling in snow after an extremely hot sauna session.

Fall or autumn is another season where you might need to adjust your itinerary. During this season, expect a lot of raining. It may be impossible to do common tourist activities.

Traditional Sauna: Vana-Kalamaja 9a, 10414 Tallinn

Phone:+372 627 1811

Luckily, there are still other ways to enjoy Tallinn during autumn.

Go on bus tours

Walk and bike tours are what tourists often go on when they are in Tallinn. But, this may be hard to do during autumn. There are great chances of rain that you would not want to get soaked in.

Instead, why not go on bus tours? These tours are available all-year-round, but they are more popular during autumn. You will be able to see the beautiful city without the great risk of getting sick during your vacation.

Take a walk around the city

If the weather would be wonderful, take a walk in different parks around the city. You will see the beauty of Tallinn and its streets covered in autumn leaves.

Wait for the sunrise and sunset

The sun sets earlier and rises later in Tallinn during autumn. This will give you a perfect chance to marvel at the wonderful colored autumn skies in the city.

The best viewing spot for sunrises would be the viewing platforms on Toompea Hill. For the best view of the sunset, head on over to Pirita and wait for the sunset by the beach.

Go coffee shop hopping

You might be able to go to a few coffee shops around Tallinn during other seasons. But, the best season to enjoy a nice hot cup of coffee would be autumn.

The temperature is not too hot or too cold, so you will be able to enjoy your coffee fully. There are so many cafés in town, so you can go from one café to the other.

These are just sample itineraries for your 3-day Tallinn trip. You can make your own itinerary based on your interests, preferred activities, and the time of the year you will visit.

Danish King's garden Monk statue

15

Conclusion

I want to thank you for reading this book! I sincerely hope that you received value from it!

If you received value from this book, I want to ask you for a favour. Would you be kind enough to leave a review for this book on Amazon?

accounting, officially permitted, or otherwise, qualified services. If advice is necessary, legal or professional, a practiced individual in the profession should be ordered.

– From a Declaration of Principles which was accepted and approved equally by a Committee of the American Bar Association and a Committee of Publishers and Associations.

© *OpenStreetMap contributors*

Credit : https://www.openstreetmap.org/copyright
  (User: Riggwelter at wts wikivoyage)

Printed in Great Britain
by Amazon